My Journal

Name: _____

Return to: _____

Book #: _____ Date: _____

hancock house

Note from the author/publisher:

This series of Journals is embellished with photos from my files or various Hancock House titles. The fine line drawings are by *Susan ImBaumgarten* from *Rocky Mountain Wildlife* and *Birds of British Columbia*.

Hancock House has published over 500 titles on the North West over the years for your enjoyment and reference. Most are still in print, or the updated versions of them are, and are available from your local store or directly from www.hancockhouse.com.

I have personally selected the material in this series to reflect our incredible west coast native cultural and wildlife diversity and I hope the images remind you of your visit, and stimulate another trip soon. You might also consider giving these journals to friends to introduce them to our spectacular area.

ISBN 0-88839-631-7 Journal [eagle cover]
ISBN 0-88839-634-1 Journal [flower cover]
Copyright © 2006 Hancock House Publishers

All rights reserved. No part of this publication may be reproduced, stored in a retrieval system or transmitted, in any form or by any means, electronic, mechanical, photocopying, recording, or otherwise, without the prior written permission of Hancock House Publishers.

Printed in Indonesia — T.K. PRINTING
Production: Laura Michaels
Design & photography is by David Hancock, unless otherwise credited.

Published simultaneously in Canada and the United States by

HANCOCK HOUSE PUBLISHERS LTD.
19313 Zero Avenue, Surrey, B.C. Canada V3S 9R9
(604) 538-1114   Fax (604) 538-2262

HANCOCK HOUSE PUBLISHERS
1431 Harrison Avenue, Blaine, WA U.S.A. 98230-5005
(604) 538-1114   Fax (604) 538-2262

Website: www.hancockhouse.com
Email: sales@hancockhouse.com

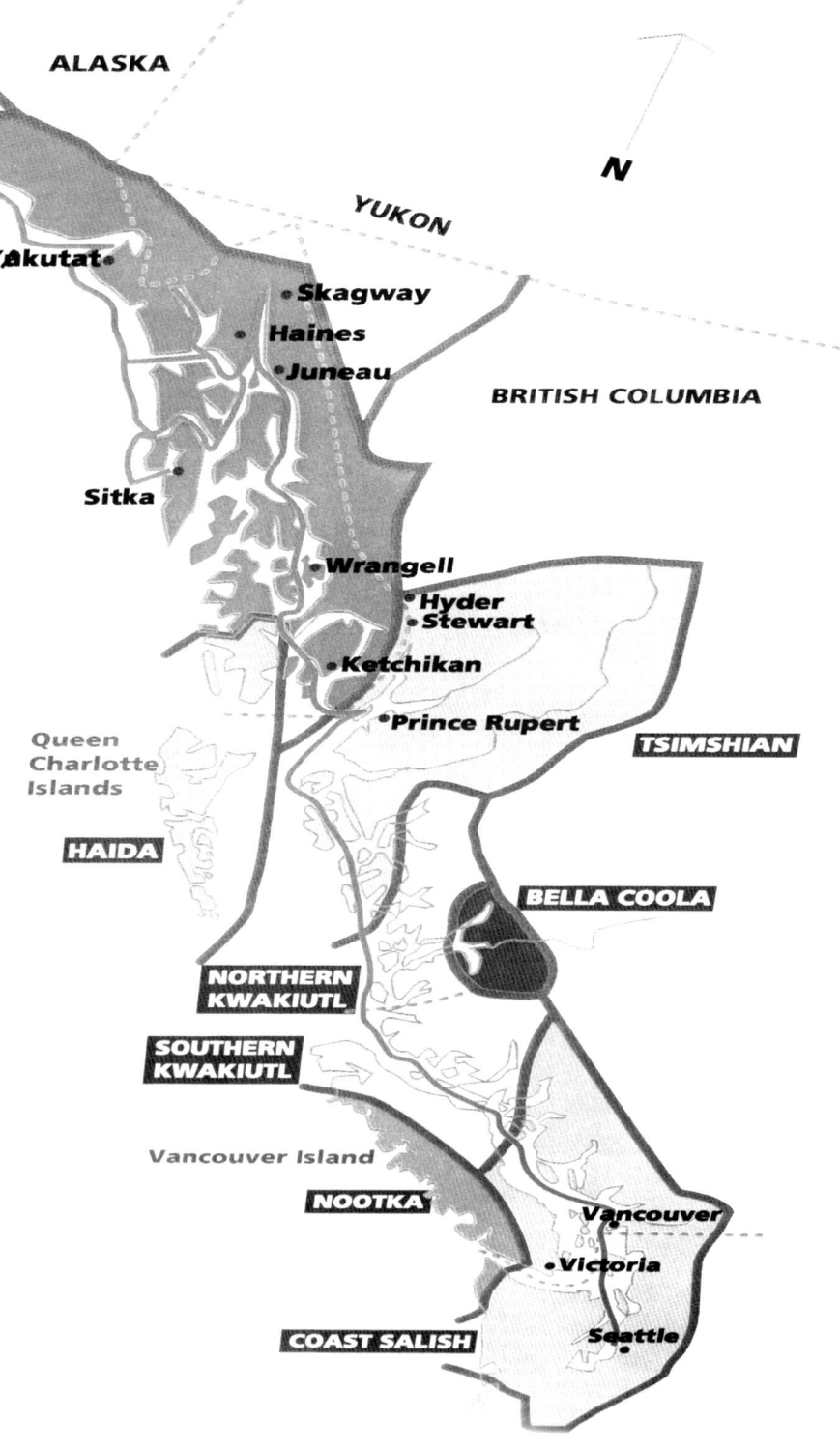

Double Transformation Mask

Bella Coola Pole
from *Art of the Totem*

Cougar

Wild Rose

Haida House Frontal

Shaman

Black Bear Cub

Black Bear with a lucky catch—from *Bears of the North*   Photo: *Steven Kazlowski*

Snowy Owl—from *Birds of North America*

Snowy Owl

Pileated Woodpecker

Nest Hole of Pileated Woodpecker with young

Coast Salish Sxwaixwe Mask by Simon Charlie
from *Coast Salish Art & Culture*

Coast Salish Pole—from *Coast Salish Art & Culture*

Lily of the Valley

Peregrine Falcon—from *Birds of North America*

Wolf

Orca—from *The Awesome Orca* Photo: Captain Larry

Humpback Whale—from *Wildlife of the North*   Photos: Steven Kazlowski

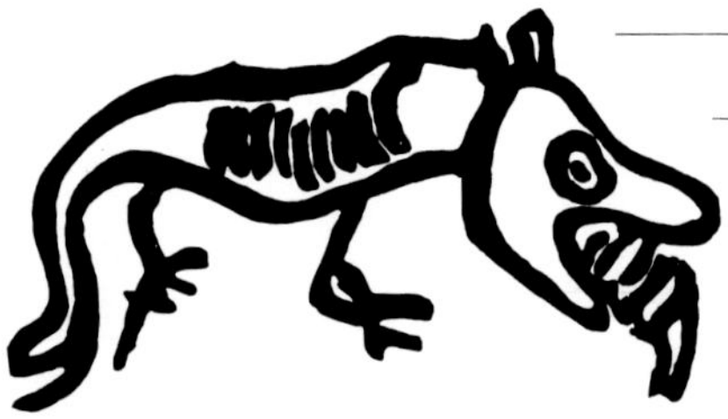

Grizzly Bears

Grizzly Bear Cub—from *Rocky Mountain Wildlife* Photo: Brian Wolitski

North West Coast Masks

White Spirit Bear with black cub—from *Bears of the North*
Photo: Steven Kazlowski

White Spirit Bear with cubs—from *White Spirit Bear*
Photo: Joe Mandur

Barrows Goldeneye

White-tailed Ptarmigan

Cougar lying in wildflower meadow

Moose

Cow and Calf

Haida Weaver Hat—from *Western Indian Basketry*

Haida Pole—from *Haida Art & Culture*

Spotted Skunk

Striped Skunk

This is not the fox-trot, but the coyote shuffle—from *Guide to Wildlife of the Rockies*

Model of Shaman's Grave

Tlingit Grave Houses

Bald Eagle—from *The Bald Eagle of Alaska, B.C. and Washington*

Pika

Mountain Chickadee

Boreal Chickadee

Sasquatch Portrait—from *Meet the Sasquatch*
By Christopher Murphy

Sasquatch—from *The Bigfoot Film Controversy* Roger Patterson film still #352

Yellow-eyed Grass

Hairy Cinquefoil

Kwakiutl Pole—from *Indians of the Northwest Coast*

Magpies feeding on road kill

Double-crested Cormorants—from *Birds of North America*

Stone Maul

Wedge

Knife—all from *Indian Art and Culture*

D Adz

Starfish—from *Tidepool and Reef*

Haida Mortuary Poles

Dogwood, British Columbia's Provincial Flower   Photo: Dana Visalli
from *Coastal Wildflowers*

Hounds Tongue Hawkweed

Photo: Walt Lockwood

Pink Monkey Flower—from *Mountain Wildflowers*

Northwestern Waterthrush

Many-spined Prickly-pear—from *Dryland Wildflowers*   Photo: Dana Visalli

Foxglove—from *Coastal Wildflowers*

Scarlet Gilia—from *Dryland Wildflowers*

Salmon Trap for small stream—from *Indian Art and Culture*

Fish Basket—from *Indian Art and Culture*

Sandhill Crane Chicks—from *Rocky Mountain Wildlife* Photo: Mia Hancock

Wood Lily

Mountain Avens

Wood-grub Child—*fom Art of the Totem*

Nootka Pole—from *Totem Poles of the Northwest*

Haida Memorial Pole

Nootka Hat

Steller Sea Lions

Steller Sea Lion—from *Guide to Western Wildlife*

Order more journals from
www.hancockhouse.com *or* **1-800-938-1114**

ISBN 0-88839-631-7

ISBN 0-88839-634-1

Art of the Totem
Marius Barbeau
0-88839-618-X
5½ x 8½, sc, 64 pages

**Haida:
Their Art and Culture**
Leslie Drew
0-88839-621-X
5½ x 8½, sc, 96 pages

**Coast Salish:
Their Art and Culture**
Reg Ashwell
0-88839-620-1
5½ x 8½, sc, 96 pages

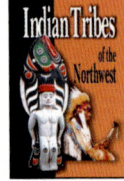
**Indian Tribes
of the Northwest**
Reg Ashwell
0-88839-619-8
5½ x 8½, sc, 96 pages

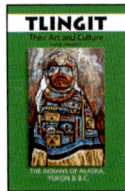
**Tlingit:
Their Art and Culture**
David Hancock
0-88839-530-2
5½ x 8½, sc, 96 pages

Meet the Sasquatch
*Chris Murphy, John Green,
Thomas Steenburg*
0-88839-573-6
8½ x 11, sc, 240 pages

Wildlife of the North
Steven Kazlowski
0-88839-590-6
8½ x 11, sc, 47 pages

**Bald Eagle of Alaska,
BC and Washington**
David Hancock
0-88839-536-1
5½ x 8½, sc, 96 pages

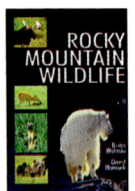
Rocky Mountain Wildlife
Brian Wolitski, David Hancock
0-88839-567-1
8½ x 11, sc, 96 pages

**Northwest Coastal
Wildflowers**
*Dana Visalli, Derek Ditchburn,
Walter Lockwood*
0-88839-518-3
5½ x 8½, sc, 96 pages

**Northwest Mountain
Wildflowers**
*Dana Visalli, Derek Ditchburn,
Walter Lockwood*
0-88839-516-7
5½ x 8½, sc, 96 pages

**Northwest Dryland
Wildflowers**
*Dana Visalli, Derek Ditchburn,
Walter Lockwood*
0-88839-518-3
5½ x 8½, sc, 96 pages

**Guide to Rocks and
Minerals of the Northwest**
Stan & Chris Leaming
0-88839-053-X
5½ x 8½, sc, 32 pages

**Guide to
Western Mushrooms**
J.E. Underhill
0-88839-031-9
5½ x 8½, sc, 32 pages

**Wild Harvest:
Edible Plants of the
Pacific Northwest**
Terry Domico
0-88839-022-X
5½ x 8½, sc, 86 pages

**Northwestern
Wild Berries**
J.E. Underhill
0-88839-027-0
5½ x 8½, sc, 48 pages

Order all books from your local store or directly from:
www.hancockhouse.com • 1-800-938-1114